GW00645205

This Is What We Sang
by Gavin Kostick

LAGAN PRESS

Published by
Lagan Press
Unit 45
30-50 Distillery Street
Belfast, BT12 5BJ
www.lagan-press.org.uk

© Gavin Kostick, 2009

ISBN: 978-1-904625-74-8

For performing rights, please contact:
Kabosh Theatre Company
Imperial Buildings
72 High Street
Belfast, BT1 2BE

This Is What We Sang is the culmination of a two-year process. Kabosh are grateful to the following funding bodies for assistance in delivering this project:

THE PETER AND MICHAEL
HILLER CHARITABLE TRUST

Contents

Kabosh Production Programme   *7*

Script of 'This Is What We Sang' by Gavin Kostick   *23*

'The Lamplighters' by Jo Egan   *61*

'Kol Isha – The Voice of a Woman' by Katy Radford   *71*

Kabosh present
This Is What We Sang

By **Gavin Kostick**

Directed by **Paula McFetridge**

Music composed and directed by **Neil Martin**

Cast and Production

Lev - **Lalor Roddy**
Hannah - **Laura Hughes**
Siss - **Jo Donnelly**
Bill - **Paul Kennedy**
Saul - **Alan Burke**

Set Designer - **Stuart Marshall**
Costume Designer - **Rosie Moore**
Lighting Designer - **Conleth White**
Voice Coach - **Peter Ballance**

Production Manager - **Elaine Barnes**
Stage Manager - **Monica McNally**
Production Assistant - **Ryan Crown**
Seamstress - **Christine Boyle**
Set Construction - **Jim Carson**
Sound Operator - **Karl Fitzpatrick**
Crew - **Lisa Marie Cooke, Caroline Curran and Anna
Donovan** *(set);* **Alan McCracken and Third Source Media**
(sound); **Mick Draine, Powerlight and Keith Shanks** *(lights).*

Producer - **Hugh Odling-Smee**
Administrator - **Fionnuala Kennedy**
Bookkeeper - **Susan Neil**
Print Design - **Atto**

'This Is What We Sang' premiéred as part of the Ulster Bank
Belfast Festival at Queen's in the Belfast Synagogue on
Wednesday 21st October 2009.

Gavin Kostick
Playwright

Gavin has written over a dozen plays that have been produced in Dublin, on tour around Ireland, the UK, New York, Philadelphia and Romania. Favourite works include *The Ash Fire, The Flesh Addict, The Asylum Ball, Forked, The Medusa, An Image for the Rose Parts 1, 2* and *3.* He has written a number of works for The Gaiety School of Acting, the latest being *Olive Skin, Blood Mouth.*

He is currently working on new plays for Fishamble: The New Play Company, Whiplash, and an opera with composer Raymond Deane for RTÉ Lyric FM.

Gavin is the Literary Manager for Fishamble. He works with new writers for theatre through innovative projects such as the award-winning *Whereabouts*, script development, readings and a variety of courses. Over 100 plays have been produced by writers completing courses with Fishamble.

For Dublin Fringe Festival 2007 his 5 ½ hour performance as Charlie Marlow in *Joseph Conrad's 'Heart of Darkness' Complete* received the Spirit of the Fringe award, went on to a sell-out run as part of *Reviewed* at the Ulster Bank Dublin Theatre Festival 2008 and was performed at the South Bank as part of the London Festival of Literature 2009.

Paula McFetridge
Director

Paula has been Artistic Director of Kabosh since August 2006.
For the company she has directed the premiére productions
of *Two Roads West* by Laurence McKeown in a moving
black taxi as part of Cathedral Quarter Arts Festival (CQAF)
and Féile an Phobhail 2009; *Carnival* by Lucy Caldwell in
a Spiegeltent, Custom House Square as part of Ulster Bank
Belfast Festival at Queen's 2008; *Henry & Harriet* by Carlo
Gébler as part of CQAF 2007 and Summer Sundays 2008 in
working city-centre shops and *To Have & To Hold* by Fergal
McElherron, a promenade performance in the Old Museum
Arts Centre. In addition, with Kabosh she has directed
various bespoke theatre projects for NITB, West Belfast
Tourism, Belfast City Hall, Sandy Row Tile Factory, Healing
Through Remembering, Relatives for Justice and the Trauma
Recovery Network.

Prior to Kabosh her many award-winning credits include:
Artistic Director of the Lyric Theatre 2001-2006; Artistic
Director of *convictions*, produced at Crumlin Road
Courthouse by Tinderbox Theatre Company (winner
'Best Production' 2000 at the *Irish Times*/ESB Awards);
nd Director of *Waterbabies* produced by Big Telly at the
Riverside Theatre. She also directed *North Nua* by Vincent
Higgins and *The Lottery* by Shay Linehan for RTÉ Radio 1.

Paula is also a respected theatre, radio, television and
film actress.

Neil Martin
Music Composer and Director

Belfast-born Neil grew up in a household where his parents' musical tastes ranged from Bach and Mozart to The Beatles and Ry Cooder. A cellist and an uilleann piper, he was encouraged to play both traditional and classical music from an early age. Among his teachers were piper Liam O'Flynn and cellist Richard Markson. A Music and Celtic Studies graduate of Queen's University Belfast, Neil has since enjoyed a varied and rewarding career that encompasses composition, performance and production.

Commissions in 2009 include a feature film score, *Hell's Pavement; An Indigo Sky* for string quartet; a dance project based on TS Eliot's *Four Quartets* and television work. Other major commissions include *ossa* (2007), a choral symphony to mark the 400th anniversary of The Flight of the Earls and composed for orchestra, solo boy treble and 120 voice chorus; *no tongue can tell* (2004), a major work for uilleann pipes and symphony orchestra featuring Liam O'Flynn as soloist; *Soundings* (2007), a chamber trio for Lyric FM and *Oilean na Mabh* (2006), a song cycle for Maighread Ni Dhomhnaill and the West Ocean String Quartet. The quartet's most recent CD *The Guiding Moon*, with The Chieftains' Matt Molloy on flute, was released to huge acclaim at home and abroad with rave reviews in New York, Chicago, France and Australia.

Neil has composed and directed music extensively for theatre (Field Day, Tinderbox, Dubbeljoint, Prime Cut, Lyric, Gaiety, OMAC and Ulster Youth), notably Stephen Rea's award-winning production of *Northern Star* (1998). Composition for television, film and radio includes Trevor Griffiths' RTS award-winning television drama *Food for Ravens* (1997); various short dramas; dozens of documentaries and series for BBC, Ch4, and RTÉ, and many radio dramas.

Lalor Roddy
Lev

Lalor's previous theatre credits include *This Piece of Earth* (Ransom); *To Have and to Hold* (Kabosh); *The Home Place, The Lonesome West, John Bull's Other Island, Paradise, The Weir* (TMA 'Best Actor' nomination), *Over the Bridge* and *A Doll's House* (Lyric Theatre, Belfast); *Lay Me Down Softly, In a Little World of Our Own* (Winner 'Best Actor' *Irish Times* Awards) and *Defender of the Faith* (Peacock); *The Freedom of the City* (Abbey Theatre and Lincoln Centre, New York); *Place of Pigs* (Prime Cut); *The Tempest* and *Observe the Sons of Ulster Marching Towards the Somme* (Abbey); *Hard to Believe* (Bickerstaff); *Pentecost, Gibraltar Strait* and *convictions* (Tinderbox); *Measure for Measure, Shadows, King Baby* and *Amphibians* (RSC).

His film and television credits include *Hunger, Five Minutes of Heaven, Cherrybomb, Boy Eats Girl, All Things Bright and Beautiful, Pulling Moves, 81, City of Amber* and *Between the Lines.*

Laura Hughes
Hannah

Laura is a graduate of Queen's University, Belfast. Her recent theatre work includes *A Very Weird Manor, New Year's Eve Can Kill You, Wonderful Tennessee, Annie – the Musical, The Sound of Music* and *Season's Greetings* for the Lyric. Other credits include *Women on the Verge of HRT* (Andrew's Lane, Dublin) in which she played Vera; *Alice: the Musical* (Purpose Built Musicals); *School for Scandal* and *Blood*

Wedding (Bruiser Theatre Company); *Emma* (Storytellers Theatre Company) and *Feast of Lupercal* (Belfast Theatre Company Tour) for which she was nominated as 'Best Supporting Actress' in the ESB/*Irish Times* Theatre Awards. Most recently she has been co-deviser and director of *Theatresquad* for Replay Productions.

Her film and television credits include *Small Island, 50 Dead Men Walking, The Clinic, Be More Ethnic, Sunday Bloody Sunday, The Most Fertile Man in Ireland* and *Blackwater Lightship*. Her radio work includes *School for Hope, Our Lady of Sligo* and *Pentecost* (BBC Radio 4); *Twin Trouble* and *Tricycles* (BBC Radio 3). Laura has also narrated various BBC and Channel 4 documentaries as well as numerous adverts on radio and UTV.

Jo Donnelly
Siss

Jo graduated from RADA in 2000. She last appeared with Kabosh in *Henry & Harriet*. Her other theatre credits include *Striking Distance, Flaming Fables, Almost Human* and *Bathtime* (Replay Productions); *The Factory Girls* and *The Snow Queen* (Lyric Theatre Belfast); *Who's Harry* (Old Museum Arts Centre); *Watermark* (Crucible Sheffield and Waterfront Belfast); *Can't Pay? Won't Pay!* (Derby Playhouse) and, most recently, *The Chronicles of Long Kesh* (Edinburgh Festival) which won *The Stage* Award for 'Best Ensemble'.

Her radio credits include *Ulster Way* and *The Real Charlotte* (BBC NI).

Paul Kennedy
Bill

Paul graduated from the University of Ulster Theatre
Studies Department in 2002. His theatre experience includes
Carnival (Kabosh); *The Session* (Dubbeljoint); *Diary of a
Hunger Striker* (Aisling Ghear); *Heroes with Their Hands in the
Air, Rat in the Skull* and *Flight* (Derry Playhouse); *Catherine
Medbh* (Miniaturists); *As You Like It* and *The Waiting List*
(Jigsaw).

His film and television credits include *Five Minutes of Heaven,
50 Dead Men Walking, Cherrybomb, Omagh, Occupation,
Endgame, Rip and the Preacher, Maru, Give My Head Peace,
Davy Jones, Teethgrinder* and *A Funny Thing Happened on the
Way Through the Troubles.*

Alan Burke
Saul

Alan formed the group Afterhours in 1986. He caroused
across Europe, America and Canada with them for the
following 10 years, recording three albums, *Afterhours* (1988),
Hung Up and Dry (1990) and *Up to Here* (1992).

Alan has two solo CDs to his credit: *On the Other Hand*
(1997) and *Tip of the Tongue* (2000). In 2002 he made a
library recording for the BMG label alongside Cathal Hayden,
Maurice Lennon, Jim McGrath and James Blennerhasset. In
2003 he produced and performed with the Donegal singer
Bríd Ní Mhaoileoin *Ar Mhuin na Muice,* and the following
year recorded *The Eagle's Whistle* with the group Airla
featuring the Derry piper Joe McHugh. Alan collaborated with

Kane O'Rourke on *The Jolly Tinker* (2007) and appeared on Geraldine Bradley's CD *From the Rising Spring; Cloch Fhuráin*. Alongside his solo performances, Alan plays with the band At First Light featuring John McSherry, Francis McIlduff, Dónal O'Connor and Ruben Bada; they are currently recording.

In addition Alan performed in *The Session* (Dubbeljoint Productions); presented *Ceol Ón gCroí* (TG4), looking at historic events in Irish history through song; and created and performed *Belfast: City of Sin* (a subterranean musical walking tour of Belfast) with Gearoid MacLochlainn for the Open House Festival 2009.

Stuart Marshall
Set Designer

Stuart was resident designer at the Lyric Theatre 1994-1998; during that time and since, he has designed over fifty shows there including *Pictures of Tomorrow, The Crucible, Of Mice and Men, La Chunga, A Night in November, Charlotte's Web, Arms and the Man, To Be Sure* and *The Hypochondriact*.

In 1992 he was one of the four original members of Prime Cut (then Mad Cow) Productions, and his work for them has included *A Place with the Pigs, Criminal Genius/Problem Child, Gagarin Way, American Buffalo* and, most recently, *The Heights* by Lisa McGee. In 2000 Stuart designed *Shalom Belfast* by Rebecca Bartlett for Replay Productions, a theatre-in-education play telling the story of Jewish immigrants to Belfast. He was also Design Consultant for the Holocaust Memorial Day National Commemorative Event, which took place in Belfast in 2004.

Stuart has also designed for many other companies including *The Winners* and *Transparency* (Ransom Productions); *The Diary of Anne Frank* and *The Field* (Bardic Theatre); *Family Plot* and *The Chairs* (Tinderbox); *The Country Boy* and *Bog People* (Big Telly); *The Tailor's Daughter* (Belfast Festival 2007) and *Women on the Verge of HRT* (GBL Productions).

Rosie Moore
Costume Designer

Rosie has designed and made costumes for various theatre productions including *1974 - The End of Year Show* (Lyric Theatre) and *Who Dares to Speak* (Lynx Productions). She was Costume Assistant with Kabosh on *carnival*. Her television and film experience includes *Give My Head Peace* and the feature film *Waz*. She designs and makes costumes for carnivals such as The Lord Mayor's Parade and the Lantern Parade with the Beat Initiative, for whom she also facilitates workshops as an Artist in the Community, helping children and adults make costumes and props for various carnivals. Rosie has also worked as a stagecraft tutor for Starburst Children's Theatre School and as a Fashion and Design tutor for Belfast Metropolitan College.

She has a vintage fashion business called Lulu Rose selling men's and women's vintage clothing and accessories through her website (www.lulurose.co.uk) as well as at various fairs, markets and fashion events, the most recent being Frock Around the Clock Vintage Fair, Holiday Inn Belfast. She also has her own label of unique clothing and accessories called Aubergine Lining, which she makes using recycled materials and vintage elements.

Conleth White
Lighting Designer

Conleth has toured to Belgrade, Taiwan, Denmark and the UK with Big Telly's swimming-pool production of *The Little Mermaid* and lit their latest water-based show *Sinbad*. Also for Big Telly he lit *Puckoon, The Country Boy, The Shadow of the Glen, The Tinker's Wedding, Well of the Saints, The Picture of Dorian Gray* and *Bog People*. For Kabosh he previously lit *To Have & To Hold* in the Old Museum. For Green Shoot/GBL productions he lit *The Chronicles of Long Kesh, The Interrogation of Ambrose Fogarty, Women on the Verge of HRT* and *Lay Up Your Ends* in the Grand Opera House, Belfast and *A Night in November* at the Olympia, Dublin and Trafalgar Studio One, London.

He designed the set and lighting for the ART(NI) production of Hugh Leonard's *Da* and the lighting for their recent production of *Juno and The Paycock*. Other recent lighting credits include *Climb, The Boy Soldier* and *Riddley Walker* (Red Kettle, Waterford); *1974 - The End of Year Show, Days of Wine and Roses* and *The Hypochondriact* (Lyric, Belfast); *Dogshow* in the Galway and Kilkenny Arts Festivals and set and lighting for *Fido* in the Dublin Fringe 2007 (both by Garrett Keogh); *The Duke of Hope* (Irish tour, Tinderbox); *The Liverpool Boat* by Marie Jones & Maurice Bessman (Red Lead, Docker's Club, Belfast); *Dublin Carol* (Everyman Palace, Cork); for Axis Ballymun *The Consequences of Lightning, Walking the Road* (also in Ieper, Belgium) and *The Townlands of Brazil* (also in Teatr Polksi, Wroclaw); *Macbeth* in Crumlin Road Gaol for Replay Productions and *War of the Roses III* and *Spartacus: Highway to Hell* for Whiplashfights.

He helped produce and design *Four Last Things* for Lisa Tierney-Keogh in Absolut Fringe 2009 at Smock Alley. Recent dance includes lighting and co-production of *Tundra* in The Empty Space, Dublin (with Anne Gilpin and Ian Wilson (Triptych)); *The Nutcracker Suite* in the Helix for RTÉ's Ballet Chancers and *The Four Quartets* for Maiden Voyage.

Peter Ballance
Voice Coach

Peter qualified as an accent coach in 2001 after completing his Masters in Voice Studies at Central School of Speech and Drama, London. Since then he has worked on many productions for stage and television providing advice on accents and voice for Kabosh, Bruiser, Tinderbox, BBC NI, Big Telly and Prime Cut amongst others.

He is also involved with Queen's University's BA in Drama and their Centre of Excellence in the Performing Arts. Peter is the new coordinator of the BTec National Diploma in Performing Arts at Southern Regional College.

Peter is also an experienced theatre, radio, television and film actor.

Elaine Barnes
Production Manager

Elaine has worked extensively throughout Northern Ireland as a Stage Manager and was short-listed for an SMA Individual Award in 2008. She previously worked with Kabosh on *Carnival* by Lucy Caldwell, *Henry & Harriet* by Carlo Gébler and *To Have & To Hold* by Fergal McElherron. Her other theatre credits include *Johnny Meister and The Stitch* (Jigsaw Theatre Co.); *A Night in November* starring Patrick Kielty, *The Interrogation of Ambrose Fogarty* and *Women on the Verge of HRT* (GBL Productions); *Caught Red Handed, Girls and Dolls* and *The Duke of Hope* (Tinderbox Theatre Company); *Observe the Sons of Ulster Marching Towards the Somme, Christmas Eve Can Kill You, True West, The Lonesome West* and *The Snow Queen* (Lyric Theatre, Belfast); *The Blind Fiddler* (Lyric Theatre, Grand Opera House and Edinburgh Fringe Festival); *La Bohème* and *The Gala Evening 2008* (Castleward Opera); *The Liverpool Boat* (Red Lead Arts); *The Submarine Man* (Upstate Theatre); *Danny and the Deep Blue Sea* (Brass Neck Productions) and, most recently *The Chronicles of Long Kesh* (Green Shoot Productions 2008 & 2009 tours).

Monica McNally
Stage Manager

Monica graduated from Queen's University in 2006 with a BA Hons in Theatre; since then she has worked in various roles within the industry. Her Stage Management credits include *The Country Boy, Bog People, Sinbad, End of the Beginning/ Well of the Saints* for Big Telly Theatre Company; *Kissing Marigolds* for Red Lemon Productions; *Henry & Harriet, Two Roads West* and *The Tall Ships Project* for Kabosh.

Monica's experience as a drama facilitator has seen her work in primary and secondary schools throughout Northern Ireland. She has designed and delivered workshop programmes for companies such as Action for Children, Action Cancer and Sure Start.

Ryan Crown
Production Assistant (Student on Placement)

Ryan has just completed his A-Levels at Limavady Grammar School. He has decided to take a year out to gain work experience with a professional company before going to drama school.

Ryan has been a member of Limavady Drama Club for 12 years and has acted in several plays with Blue Eagle Productions. He hopes to follow a career in acting after drama training.

Acknowledgements

Jo Egan, Creative Producer of Kabosh 2002-2007, was a driving force in creating *This Is What We Sang*. Through conducting many hours of interviews with the Belfast Jewish Community in Belfast and England, Jo showed a dedication and commitment which assisted in this production coming to the stage.

Kabosh would like to thank the Belfast Jewish Community for their assistance and support during the creation of *This Is What We Sang*, in particular Katy Radford, Edwin Coppel, Adrian Levy, Gerald Steinberg, Michael Black and Leon Litvack who have given freely of their time enabling this project to happen. We would like to give our thanks to all the members of the community who allowed their memories of the community's life in Belfast to be recorded. Three of the interviewees have passed away since this project began, Cyril Rosenburg, Benny Matthews and Harold Ross. We remember them fondly for their invaluable contribution.

In producing *This Is What We Sang*, the following people should also be thanked: Atto, Cllr Tom Hartley, Nelson McCausland MLA, Eddie and Rosalind Price, the Peter and Michael Hiller Trust, Caroline Curran, Tinderbox, Sean Kelly, Fishamble: The New Play Company, Graeme Farrow, Michael Kelly and Nuala McGreevy at Belfast Festival.

Thanks to the ACNI Arts Development Fund, administered by Tinderbox Theatre Company, for assistance in the script development of *This Is What We Sang* through the Sectoral Dramaturgy Project. As well as the cast members, thanks to Richard Clements and Abigail McGibbon for their work on script development.

KABOSH

Founded in 1994, Kabosh is the only site-specific theatre company in the north of Ireland and is committed to challenging the notion of what theatre is and where it takes place.

Recent productions

***Two Roads West* by Laurence McKeown in a moving black taxi** *(Cathedral Quarter Arts Festival and Feilé an Phobail May and July 2009)*

***Carnival* by Lucy Caldwell in a Spiegeltent** *(Ulster Bank Belfast Festival at Queen's October 2008)*

***Henry & Harriet* by Carlo Gébler in working Belfast city-centre shops** *(Cathedral Quarter Arts Festival May and Summer Sundays 2008)*

***To Have & To Hold* by Fergal McElherron, a promenade performance in the Old Museum Arts Centre** *(February 2007)*

As well as Bespoke Theatre Events for Healing Through Remembering, Arts & Business, Relatives for Justice, Northern Ireland Tourist Board, the Trauma Recovery Network, AV Browne, Good Relations Southern Clusters and Belfast City Hall.

Kabosh, Imperial Buildings, 72 High Street, Belfast, BT1 2BE t: (028) 9024 3343, e: info@kabosh.net, w: www.kabosh.net

Kabosh Board

Alison McCrudden *(Chair)*
Jenny Cooke
Mary Jordan
David Lewis
Ciaran Mackel
Orla McKeagney
Lindsay Robinson

Artistic Director: **Paula McFetridge**
Creative Producer: **Hugh Odling-Smee**
Administrator: **Fionnuala Kennedy**
Bookkeeper: **Susan Neil**

'With Kabosh expect the unexpected' *(Irish News)*

This Is What We Sang
by Gavin Kostick

Lev

Hannah

Bill

Siss

Saul

Yom Kippur.

Enter Lev, Hannah, Siss, *to the edge of the playing area, predominantly in white (but not obsessively so). Enter* Bill *in a suit, separate. They are barefoot. They stand waiting. They don't engage with each other. Enter* Saul *singing the Kol Nidre (the prayer before evening service).*

The story is told through the stages of:

Repentance.

Sacrifice.

Forgiveness.

All these are both in relation to God and man. The characters are speaking to God (or to their own sense of the divine) and man.

The characters all understand what they are being asked for, but don't necessarily agree with it.

Please note that the text of the play that appears in this programme may be changed during the rehearsal process and so appear in a slightly different format during the performance.

Section 1. *Repentance.*

[LEV *is in his prime.*]

LEV: The Gates of Prayer are open. When I was a child, my father used to say that at Yom Kippur, The Gates of Prayer are open and I used to imagine a big, bright, wind blowing through golden gates. He said it in Yiddish of course. [*repeats in Yiddish*] Di toyern fan tfile zaynen ofn.

Repentance? Well, for myself I am not now in so good a position to repent – not the things I have done anyway. They are all done and that's that and I won't deny them. But here I am again to welcome my daughter home, and one wonders, well, should it have been done differently?

What should one repent in life? The things not done? Left undone? A talent left unused? A gift not celebrated? A life not really lived? To not use a gift, I think that is to be repented. But even this is perhaps not so simple.

See, my brother, Saul, now he had a gift. He could sing, and you know what – it made him poor all his life. Because why? Because there is an obligation to a gift. To serve it, use it. It is given and it would be a crime against God, against Nature, not to. So Saul sang, he grew his beard and he was our khazn, our Cantor you know, in the shul on Great Victoria Street. Saul sang the psalms on the Shabbat. While he sang you would think this man is happy because he is open to the divine.

But otherwise? Feh, – he did get paid, he was not in, you know, desperate poverty. No, but he went through his life with nothing more than would take him to the end of the week – and sometimes not even that. And it is a piece of grit in the mind to be always poor.

And me, what gifts I had – did I use them? Can I repent of what I did with them? Will my daughter open her arms to me once all is known? Well, perhaps if you would listen, then perhaps you can decide what should be done with me, when the Gates of Prayer are closed.

I am Lev. Lev. I started things here in Belfast. I had a good life. Really. I left my children better than my father left me, is that not good? I left a son in New York and a son in Cleveland, [*hint of a pause*] and a daughter. And I had grandchildren who looked well-fed and round- faced, in the photographs sent back – is that not good? I left a wife and … well.

Let's see, in the year 1895 and at the age of eighteen years, myself and my good brother Saul left our shtetl and sought a new life in the America. [*Breathes*] Now that was a great start! We were going to exchange the wooden houses and the gloomy pine forests of my ancestors for the sparkling brownstones of New York!

Already you are ahead of me, this is not New York – this is Belfast, what are you doing here? – It's the old story, yes it is, myself and Saul had tickets for the America. But of course we were swindled. We were all swindled and landed short and we found ourselves in a place called Hull. That's in the North of England. Hull. Oh, I can see you shudder – Hull, it sounds terrible, what a dreadful place Hull must be, a stinky, smoky place, worse than Manchester, ough – but not at all, not at all, Hull was pretty enough. But I could get no business started there. Whenever I tried to get going, I would hear – "ho, you there, Farshtinkener, (stinker) this is my patch, gay avek, find yourself somewhere new". So I asked about a bit for somewhere new, and I was told Belfast, Belfast a man can make a living there, and so I went, and this must have been about, 1897.

What did I see when I arrived? I saw the docks of course and the shipyards. And I saw the Customs House. It had these gods carved on it and a man next to me: an educated man he must have been, he picked them out and said they were the gods of Manufacture, Commerce, Industry and oy, Peace, Peace of course. So I thought great, this is what I want. A city whose gods are Manufacture, Commerce, Industry and Peace. This is a good sign.

You see now, my true gift, such as it was, was to make money. If I had been Saul, I would have spent my days singing and I would have been poor. Or Benny, dear Benny. Benny and his poor hands. Benny Rosen he was. I met him in Belfast, another from Latvia. He was a heymisher mensch – a man you could get on with. He had a little house in the Carlisle Circus area. He was a cabinet-maker. Very good with his hands, another gifted man you see. Now Benny had a business making furniture, good quality, dining tables, writing desks. Very good. And he was going bust – for why? Because the people could not afford his prices. Not enough of them anyway. He had a workshop near Donegall Square, and it would break your heart to see all these lovely pieces all stacked up to the ceiling and not selling.

So I called in to his little house one day – you could just call on anyone in the community in those days – and I sat him down and I said look, Mr Rosen, we will be partners if you want, I will run the business, you will make the furniture and we will both be rich.

Benny made quality dining tables that would cost a person £5, and that was a lot. And he would use very good veneers in that. Walnut say or cedar. Absolutely the best. But I'm sorry to say this, but it's a fact of human nature that very few people really know good from bad. Not really. Oh people pretend they do – oh Mozart, oh Mahler how marvellous – but really they have no clue. So, apart from a few connoisseurs, like Benny, walnut looks a lot like apple, or cherry, or really it all looks just like wood. So, I said to Benny, look, we'll get your cost down to £2 a table and then we'll sell them at £3. Use cheaper veneers, off cuts; I'll get them for you. You have to remember they were fitting out whole ships in the docks and if a man paid the right person down there, well a consignment could be got... you understand. And we had a big argument over that when Benny found out how I was getting the wood, and to be fair to Benny – and he had the talent – he said it would be better to make a modern, simpler range with no veneers at all without any dodgy dealings that could come in at £2. And he made me up a sample, and oh, I knew I could sell a thousand, they were so simple and clean and modern.

You look at me and you see this old-fashioned man and maybe you think, how old-fashioned things were in his day, and how strange the world must have looked in brown and white, his English sits in the back of his throat – but no! We were young and modern and everything was new and colourful, and so Benny started to make this lovely clean new style.

Meshane mokem, meshane mazl. [*New place, new luck*].

Now, here's the really clever thing I did. Even at £3, a lot of people who wanted a nice dining table with matching chairs could not afford it. So I did this: I gave them the dining table and agreed a very reasonable rate of repayment over three years, which was a small amount weekly. You see. Maybe 6 pennies a week, which added up to £3 10 shillings over three years. And this was not a swindle at all. No, a good hard-working man could come home to a lovely meal with his family and have the benefit of good furniture at a rate that didn't hurt them.

Later we made beds and I had Marky Coppel supply the mattresses.

I had a book I kept all the details in. Once we got going I kept it all proper. Benny was right about that – there was no need for anything underhand: I made sure we paid our taxes and everything. It was all above the board. Then I realised the value in being a good citizen, you know, parnose a healthy living, for the family, and for the good of all. And so the city regarded us as good, legitimate businessmen, so that if a person defaulted – didn't pay us – I could take him to court. There was no need for anything unpleasant, any heavy stuff you might say, the law would look after us. Did I feel bad taking people to court? – No, not a bit. Nothing to repent there. How would it be fair on all my good customers if I let the bad apples away? No, as long as everyone paid, we could keep our prices low, and everyone is happy.

So Benny and I get going and really work hard, I mean it is a joy to get up every day – save the Shabbat of course – and work hard, and in five years I had a house, up on Ainsley Road. I paid £85 for it, all in cash. No mortgage. And it had three bedrooms and a study. The master bedroom, it had a bay window and Benny kindly put a seat in it.

So and I had a very good life like that, until I thought well, I'm nearly forty and I have a house with three bedrooms, and that is when I decided that a good Jew with a good business needs a good wife.

There was a family in Leeds, and this man had two daughters. How did I hear of them? – well through the Rabbi. That was the famous Rabbi Herzog at that time. That was how it was done, you know, I let it be known that I was looking for a wife, and… Was it arranged? What does this mean arranged – like in India… like we had no say? No it was really… you know, a case of finding a suitable match. And Rabbi Herzog had been brought up in Leeds. Anyway this man was big into drainage. Do you know Leeds? – Yorkshire. It's on the edge of the Pennines. Anyway it slopes and this man was cleaning up in the drainage, you know, the drains for the new estates. In fact, he got rich enough to own a coach with two horses. He had a coachman for it and everything – but he never used it in case he got lazy. He would walk to work every day, and the coachman would drive the coach, in the event he wanted it. But he never did. Later he got a Rolls Royce with a chauffeur, and he didn't use that either.

Anyway I went over to see him, and his two daughters, and oh I can't tell you how strange that was, and how nervous I felt. I mean, I was still young enough, I was an, oy, eligible bachelor, and I had a business and a house, and I had a suit on and spats and some flowers, but, you know it's a strange feeling. I had seen a photograph of course, but that's meant to tell a certain tale, to show in a flattering light – what if she's cross-eyed? Looking up the drive of this very fine house, on a misty afternoon the dog roses all blurred – and thinking maybe I shall marry one of the girls who live in this house, and maybe I won't. And maybe I shall fall in love and maybe I will not. Maybe I will fall in love.

HANNAH: I never thought I had any worth. You don't really if your father says you're worthless. So repentance, I'm very sorry, but I repent everything really. The idea is that we have done some things right and some wrong and we repent those wrong things. Well I'm afraid I think I did it all wrong. Or really was never important enough to, to sin – though I suppose I have. And Siss now, the new one coming home, my daughter. Well I got that all wrong too.

Lev? Yes. I had been worried about how old he might be – I was only twenty-three at the time, though I felt thoroughly grown up, you do at twenty-three don't you? But, I was young enough not to want to be married to some horrible, old man with grey skin and brown breath. So he called to the house – this suitor Lev. In he came. And you know, my first reaction was, very nice. This is, a man, a mentsh. He offered up the flowers and he did a little bow and he said – well he must have said something mustn't he, but I don't really remember, but I do remember his eyes twinkled. It was like we were already in on some secret joke.

So I showed him the gardens. I expect we were chaperoned, that would have been normal, but I don't remember that either. The main thing was I knew that I had to marry.

My father had come from nothing, really nothing. He had put card in the soles of his boots when they'd worn through, and he'd worked and worked and worked and given me and Lottie everything.

I'm sorry, I'm Hannah, I should have said, and my little sister is Lottie.

And, yes, my father had done very well. The story about the carriage, the one he never used – that's true. But I'm sorry to say success is not always good for the soul. He got very proud, what is it that Shakespeare calls us – "stiff necked", well that was my father, and he wanted his daughters married well. Girls were no use for him to further his business directly. That was why we were worthless. But a marriage would give him some status. I had already turned down two offers, who were daddy's business friends, and things might have been very, very unpleasant indeed if things had gone on like that. He beat us, but that was... My mother didn't think it right to interfere really. I mean, she ran the home – she was a good mother like that, always clean clothes, always food, everything right. But she... I don't think it would have occurred to her to stand up to Father.

May I be forgiven, I wanted to get away. Belfast seemed a good long way away from Leeds. You had to take a boat.

Did I love Lev straight away? No, no. But does love make a good marriage? The romantic kind of love you see in the pictures? – I'm not so sure. Much later, after my time, it became fashionable to marry for love – did that make things any better? Did we become happier? I don't know. There's a lot to be said for duty, if we could only abide it. That's it – I repent that I wasn't able to do my duty.

But like I said, Lev was a good, lively man. And he had such a fine suit on – really good cloth, well tailored. And he didn't seem old – I was really shocked later when I saw, where was it, on the marriage contract, that he was 39. Of course I should have thought, why wasn't he off at war? The Great War was on at the time. But I just thought they hadn't conscripted him because business was vital to the war effort or something, not that he was too old. If you had seen him, you would never have thought he was 39. He was so lively, he jumped about the place, but elegant too, you could see the man could dance. A lovely little moustache. And he was so interested in things – what was this tree, who had planted it, what nest was that, were there eggs in it, who had owned the house before us, and he listened to my answers, and my father, I don't think, had really listened before. I don't think it occurred to him to listen to me or Lottie ever but Lev did, and then he started talking about his brother Saul, and I started talking about Lottie, and somehow I had agreed that Lev and I would be very happy, and that perhaps Lottie might come over for the wedding and meet Saul and see what she thought.

So you see, I went into it with my eyes open. Love, I don't know. The question was, could I make a good happy life in Belfast with this man, and I thought I could. I thought I could.

So, how do I explain what happened, well, well, I suppose I just say it straight out – the moment we arrived here, I fell in love with Lev's brother. Straight away.

"Hannah, this is Saul, Saul this is my wonderful wife-to-be Hannah, and this is her charming sister Lottie." Oh. Oh. I want to live with you forever.

Saul had met us at the docks. And it was like a joke, his face was a touch wider than Lev's and his nose a touch broader, and he had a rather old-fashioned beard, and his clothes were not as good, and I took one look in his green eyes and suddenly my soul was flooded. No, no, I'll tell you exactly, exactly I first saw him profile, and he had these cheery, childlike cheeks, then he must have heard Lev, and he turned face on and it was... as if God had looked at me from behind a curtain. Is that sacrilege? Oh dear. You see I had worried so much about life, and felt so useless that it never occurred to me one might be overwhelmed by such a powerful feeling.

I felt angry at him, at Lev, at God. He had caught me by surprise. Why had he not come over? It was just fate.

I married the wrong man, so help me. But what can you say? Should I have taken Lottie aside and said, 'would you care to swap?' You take Lev and the business, I'll take Saul. It was ludicrous. I was engaged to Lev and that was that: think of the upset.

Actually – I'm somewhat misleading you. What happened was this: Saul took Lottie to one of the tea-houses in the town, and when they came back and I had her on my own I asked, sort of playfully, how had it gone? And I imagined in my head, I imagined it so hard, her saying, "Oh he's no Lev – how I wish I had your Lev." And we could have done it too! We could have swapped! We were a long way from Leeds after all. But she said, "Oh Hannah, I must be the luckiest girl alive – Saul is so lovely". So that was that. And so I repent not speaking out.

Love is all about the flesh and nothing about the flesh. Incarnate we are made flesh and carnal knowledge is of the flesh. With love one is not ashamed of the flesh because one abides the judgement of the beloved. Love and the flesh are one thing. But inside me, there was one person whom the flesh told me to love, and another whom it was my duty to love. But it is the person who you talk to in your head, whom you converse with, that you really love. And I talked to Saul.

Well, we had a joint wedding – things happened much more quickly in those days. We put up the canopy, and I married Lev and Lottie married Saul. Saul sang at the wedding. We broke the glass, and I listened to the Rabbi: 'one must be careful of a marriage for things are fragile and can be so easily destroyed', and I thought, no Rabbi, that which destroys a marriage is what is brought into the marriage, the flawed glass shatters itself, and I said to myself, I must root this love out of me – it is no good for anything. And I tried. I did try. And I repent, I repent I could not destroy my own love.

BILL: Hi, my name's Bill, I'm 37 years old. I'm from New York City, and I repent nothing. Well at least I didn't until yesterday and even then –

Look, I'm a businessman and as such I make deals. I make contractual deals in accordance with the New York legislature, and I do that for banks, which I'll tell you about in a minute.

Now, contracts are agreements between two or more parties and so long as that contract is kept, then there is nothing to repent, nothing to get guilty over, nothing to sue over – because there is no wrong-doing. Well, that's the way I view life. When I married my wife, whom I happen to love, we made a contract, and in so far as I put her above all other women, then in my marriage I have nothing to repent.

Me, maybe I sneak a glance at another woman now and then, I see some round white bosom in a magazine – so what, I'm just a man, get over it. Keep doing the right thing by the contract and then, you can open the gates and say, I have nothing to repent. Does that make me shallow? – No. It just puts my idea of complexity on the outside. Complexity is in the deals I make, not about how I feel about them. The way I see it, is that too many people concentrate on the inside, y'know – how do I feel about this, what are my emotions telling me.

So up 'til yesterday I was a very angry man, because my bank had betrayed me. I worked with Lehman Brothers and they went bankrupt – I was let go. I mean I was fired. I mean I was given a half hour to clear my desk and get out. I was one of the guys on the news with the plastic tidies, a Brooks Brothers suit and a look of shock.

Here's why I was livid. Lehman Brothers was not brought down by the dealmakers in New York – the 10,000 dealmakers of all kinds from the shoe boys to the board room, but by 120 frikking pirates in London. I do swear, I have a deal for that – it's a swear jar – Five dollars! Yes, we had an office in London where the rules on trading weren't so well defined; in fact they were very frikking lax. $10! So these 120 guys – and the traders were all guys – except the attractive London secretaries, brought the whole thing down with some God-awful stinky deals. I mean stank. And no real contracts, no real paper trails to sort the whole thing out.

Listen, I took the big bonuses and went with the kids to Disneyland Florida because that was the deal. But no New

Yorker was in on the real nuts stuff, the casino gambling. If you've been to New York you might know the Lehman Brothers Headquarters on Seventh. It's massive, confident, you know, slick. And everything's got sucked right out of it. The day they announced it, I was sick, just puked. I wasn't the only one. This huge, big network of deals just died. I mean, I never thought a machine like that could die. But it did. It was a tragedy. If you look up the website it says "Lehman Brothers Holdings Inc has filed for Bankruptcy protection in the US." "Lehman Brothers Holdings Inc has filed for Bankruptcy protection in the US." Stabbed in the back by stinky London dealers. It's like you're in shock, like after a crash I guess. No, it's like being able to look at the wreck of the Titanic standing on its end on 7th Avenue.

So that was me out. And that put pressure – bad pressure – on my contract with my wife and kids. The deal was I worked like a hopped-up baboon on amphetamines, and they got the best of everything and put up with the anxiety attacks. So now, I couldn't give them the best.

But look, to be clear about where I fit in, which I didn't think I did at all.

I'm Bill and Lev was my great-grandfather. I'm the grandson of his younger son. My grandfather was born in, er, 1921 – to Lev and Hannah – and my father was born in 1951 in Brooklyn, and I was born in Manhattan 1972. Dad's in Florida now, complaining about the humidity. His heart.

What I'm doing here is this. Three days ago I received a call. And this little scratchy voice said, "Hello Bill this is your great-aunt Siss. I'm calling from the hospice." And I said, "Aunt Siss!" you know trying like mad to work out which one she was, "great to hear from you. How are you?" and she said, "How am I? Dying that's how I am, and I want you to come over Bill." So what can you say to that, and then she talked a bit, and I worked out which one she was, that what she was saying was that she had no children, and she talked a bit about her house. And then I realised she was talking about what should she do with the house, and she was asking me to come over.

Look, I know I'm not the most sympathetic guy, but to be clear I would have come anyway, house or no house. There's a duty to family. But a windfall like that, well it couldn't have happened at a better time. I could set up on my own.

First impressions flying in, well, I didn't realise Belfast was in such a beautiful setting. Sorry for my ignorance, but the lake, the hills. It's beautiful. Old. Grander than I'd thought.

Siss is the only daughter of Lev and Hannah. I placed her in the end – she'd come over and sung at our wedding. I didn't really know her then, in fact I think I heard there was a touch of a black sheep about her. So that was the last time I saw her – before this.

I was told the time was ticking, so off to JFK, out in Belfast International, into a cab and straight to Somerton House, which is a hospice. That's a freaky place, a hospice. I expect this sounds really ignorant but I really didn't know what a hospice was. I thought it was just a kind of specialist care place or maybe a retirement home like in *The Simpsons*, but it's really where you go when there's a good chance of you dying. You know, dying. The thing was, I didn't mind the hospice, I just didn't like the idea of dying. Period. And I am going to die. That's the deal and I don't like it one bit – where did I sign up for that? I'm fairly okay with the idea that other people will die, and I've grasped the idea that I'll die one day in principle. But a hospice makes you think, makes you know, that you will really, really die. In reality. That's not great.

And I was given fair warning too, that some of the patients are just completely in denial. Like they know they're in a hospice, but – I suppose like me really – they don't know, or won't engage with what that might mean. So they don't go 'my God, I'm dying, get me a Rabbi' or a hooker or whatever. They say oh I prefer this tea to that tea, this cookie to that cookie, just like they've ever done. There was a day area I think. Warm, and it smelt of sweet tea and ham sandwiches – not good ones.

And I don't know why except I was just a ball of anger anyway after losing my job, the whole unfair thing about who dies and who lives just made me angrier. Then the cheery nurse with the clipboard said she's in here Mr Cantwell – they must have majored in cheeriness those nurses. "Look who's here to see you Sissy!" And there's this terribly old, terribly shrunken little woman, pulling on a Marlboro. Great-aunt Siss. The daughter of Lev and Hannah.

[Siss *is also in her prime.*]

Siss: Well I'll get to the end of this and you'll look back and say what was the moral of that story, and so I'll say now, the moral of this story is, "Don't smoke". That's all. And for the rest of it, well, maybe you'll find your own. All you, "I'm planning on quitting soon" sorts – repent you ever lit up.

Well. It's a strange thing to be really able to look back properly and say that was it – the best, the worst. And it's not really the big things that stand out. The Belfast Flower show – that was one of the best things, the one in Botanic Gardens. I liked that – used to enter some vegetables in it. That was a good thing in my life.

My childhood? Oh it was wonderful. Marvellous. There was the Institute you see, and they had clubs for the children, dances, and amateur drama, and card games. Always card games. And it was very lively. There were so many people about, very vigorous, it was. There was a Scout group too, but the girls weren't in that.

There was a man Harold Goldblatt. And he was very good with the amateur drama, and he went on to found a proper theatre here. And there was tennis.

Was my life limited by anti-Semitism? That's too much to say. I don't know. You see, the tennis clubs were for Protestants. They wouldn't let in Catholics or Jews. It was that kind of... bigotry I suppose. But it was just, you know, the Protestants had their clubs, so rather than cry about it, we formed our own.

It wasn't just us, you see. There were these skipping games on the street and when we were young we all played. I'd have been about seven. And these two sisters used to get me in and sing, I don't remember the rhyme properly, but it had King Billy in it. They got me to learn it and why not? So there was another little girl, called Rose, and she wanted to skip, but she had different words to the same tune. And I remember very clearly she jumped and sang her words while the sisters twirled the rope and sang their words, and at first it was funny, with everyone getting louder and louder, and me joining in with the sisters – because that was all I knew. Then somehow, it wasn't funny, and Rose was red-faced and shouting and the sisters were going faster and faster and really shouting King Billy at her, and I felt guilty and wanted to stop, but then I'd be betraying my friends. And in the end the rope was too fast and cut Rose off at the ankles, and she cried, and Rose's brothers came out to fight with the sister's brothers and then the adults came out and shouted at other adults, and I tried to say it was only a game that had gone wrong, and one of the boys said, 'what's it to you yid?'. Mother took me in. It was that sort of thing. Rose's older brother was called Jim and later... but I'll save that.

But no, anti-Semitism wasn't a big thing in my life.

I had a golden childhood. And my brothers were nine and seven years older than me, so they didn't really get in the way. I never really thought about the gap, I supposed I was just a late blessing.

Lev was a womaniser, a dreadful womaniser. At his funeral, at the shul – this was still the old one on Annesley Street, he died in 1946 – there were all these gentiles, these goy women, in black with veils, dabbing their eyes. It was funny, like something out of a movie. And some of them very glamorous too. Far too young for him, I thought. And would you believe, his bookkeeper too! She was red-eyed. His bookkeeper, a very dumpy woman, and I thought, my God, is there anyone here he did not sleep with? But at fifteen you're very disapproving of that sort of thing. At fifteen you don't believe anyone ugly or over thirty could want to have sex.

I never married. And we are told not to sleep with a man out of wedlock, and so I never slept with a man my whole life. Is that not what abiding the law means? Where is the reward for that? Repent – I regret I never slept with a man. If nothing else, to know what it was like. There, I never knew the physical love of a man.

Why should I think that one should do one's duty, when I had my father's example before me? I don't know, I just did. Maybe my life was a waste, and maybe my happiness or unhappiness is not such an important thing. My life has been like struggling along with a pair of shoes one size too tight. I don't think it ever fitted me.

I'm sorry, I find this painful at times. But it is nice to speak out for once. It's like a painful wind blowing. This is what I did, this is what I have done. But please excuse me if I find it hard to find the way through.

But my childhood was lovely, right up to fifteen years it was lovely.

We had a house with a bay window with a seat in it and a garden with a big tree. And a piano.

Lev had a brother Saul, the Cantor, and he was married to mother's sister Lottie. The two brothers married the two sisters. Now Saul couldn't afford a piano so his children used to come over and use ours. The community never paid well, but Saul was held in high regard, he used to get a free chicken every week. Later he got a phonograph and people passed on their records when they got fed up with them.

Now my brothers had proper lessons. Dolly Barnett used to come around. She was very good, very patient – but they were terrible at it. I remember them shouting at her that they didn't bloody well want to practise. Plink, plank, plunk, on and on.

But Saul's children, and me for that matter, we just sort of heard it in our heads, and with no lessons at all, just picked out the tune. It was so clear and so unfair. I used to ask myself, why did I, and Saul's children have this gift and my brothers not? Well, I thought, God withholds with one hand and gives with the other.

I overheard my mother one day, say to Lottie, with such sadness, "I have this beautiful house, and this beautiful piano, and my family can make no music." "My family can make no music." I could of course, but of course I was only a daughter and to mothers, daughters were useless. Well except that it was us who passed on the line. We had that of course.

Uncle Saul was fun. He did as little as he could as far as I could see. He used to spend his time at the Chevra Gemore and that was about it. Lottie was a seamstress. I don't know how they managed, and they kept a charity box for the poor Russian girls who needed a dowry. Maybe they ate the chickens and listened to the records and gave their money away. I don't know.

Lev and Benny got a showroom and warehouse all combined in a corner site in Donegall Square. It was a great time for them. Huge glass windows. Lev must have been, well, in his fifties's at this time – the 1930s – but he always looked well. No, I never really called him Daddy, I called him Lev. Everyone did. Anyway he had a straight back, Brylcreem in his hair. Well I think Brylcreem would have come in, it would have been beeswax or something before that. I think he must have boot-blacked it too because there was never any grey. He was an observant Jew, but some Saturdays he couldn't help going down to the shop, on some excuse or other, because the gentiles liked to shop on a Saturday, and if God struggled with business in Lev, well, He only won some of the time.

And then the war came.

Lev, in his favour, was friendly with Barney Hurwitz, and they together bought Millisle Farm, out to the East of the city. At least, Lev was in Mooney's pub when they signed the contracts and Barney got a donation out of him – like everyone: and young Jewish children were brought out from Europe, and they lived where they would have died. It was a well-run farm too – absolutely self-sufficient, a good business and saved hundreds of lives. So that stands for Lev.

But for the city – the war preparations were a joke. I mean all these reports from London and photographs and what they did to Liverpool and Coventry and the Clyde, we knew we were next. The awful Irish-man – what was his name – Lord Haw Haw – he even said there'll be Easter Eggs for Belfast this Easter. He said it. Easter Eggs meant bombs of course. And did we get ready? – no. Craigavon died without doing anything, and then Andrews came in and he was as doddery too. I mean, one day this German plane flew in daylight over a football match. Just flew around. Well, you could see then that the Luftwaffe knew there were no air defences, and with that great port, building all these ships and these planes and tanks being built here. Well it was obvious.

Lev could see what was coming and for one thing he got my brothers out of the country. They made quite a fuss about that as they were still in Queen's – playing snooker and having a very nice time, but Lev saw gloomy times here and thought it was going to be a bigger and better world in New York. So he got them into Columbia, and settled with some cousins I never knew we had, and they finished their degrees there. Mum was upset for a time.

Lev thought this a great thing – sons in New York and lawyers too – a great thing.

He joined the Home Guard – Dad's Army.

So it was the night of April 15th, 1941, and that was the night the Bosche came for us. And they were smart too, because first they bombed the reservoir, where the water came from and if you think that was foolish it wasn't, because without the water the firemen couldn't put out the fires and then they came for the city.

Oh Belfast, Belfast. I mean it's a hard town to be romantic about and a hard place to love, but by God when I saw her taken apart like that, oh it was terrible. And Liverpool, Glasgow, Newcastle, Coventry, these were hard, hard places too, and they took it all. They took all the Nazis could do, God bless them. You know, maybe I should talk about that dreadful Hitler and the Holocaust and our people, and it was all that too, but for me it was watching fire in this lovely city where I danced and played and went to school.

It was a full moon – which is what they wanted of course, so they could see. And it meant you could see too. And because there had been no drills, no shelters, we all just ran into the streets, and so a lot more of us died than needed to.

And I ran down all the way from Annesley Street to Donegall Square because I was looking for my Dad, through Carlisle Circus, past St Anne's, and pillars of wavering fire and smoke. My little pale ten-year-old legs going as fast as they could, head down bumping into people shouting and going this way and that way, and not so much thinking, but seeing Daddy, Daddy. It was just after Passover of course and you know, I was thinking of the plagues, and this rain of fire, and so I saw what happened.

So repent? Smoking. Seriously? No I don't repent. My heart is hard.

End Section 1.

Section 2. *Sacrifice.*

[SAUL *sings the afternoon prayer.*]

LEV: The other women? Oh, well, yes. I thought that might be understood. No?

I told you I was a bachelor until 39. Well I wasn't celibate – what man would be? No I had girlfriends. I had very nice girlfriends. All gentile – some Protestant, some Catholic – I didn't discriminate. But if I messed with a Jewish girl, it might have given her the wrong idea, or ruined her reputation. I went with girls where there was no question about marriage and I was clear about that.

But it was no hole-in-the-corner stuff. No, I took them out to dinner, The Carlton, went dancing. I gave them nice gifts. I was upfront about it.

Look, some men fall in love, once, and that's the woman for them, and they're happy – like Saul. Well, I was never like that, I liked women, they liked me.

After I married Hannah, I did think, well that's it Lev, settle down now, but well, you can't teach an old dog new tricks, so it wasn't too long before, you know. You see, some people can sacrifice one part of their life for another – not me.

This is what I was saying about a gift. My gifts were business and women. Why should God give me these things and ask me to sacrifice them in life? No.

Now with Hannah it was difficult because though, no it was not love, she was my wife, my own baleboste, and had to be treated well. I wanted her to be happy. She was always the most important woman in my world. So the arrangement I came to with myself was this. I made up a little apartment above the shop and that way, made sure that nothing ever came into our house. But I didn't try to hide things either. It was an arrangement. Understood.

I remember when the boys were very young – before Siss – we went to Portstewart for the week. You know the beach there, and it was so lovely. With the little cliffs and green fields above and just the faintest breeze. It felt like God Himself created this place in case He should desire for a holiday. I say we went for the week, but I was going back early for work and to see this

nice lady who ran a haberdasher's. Anyway, I was looking at
the boys run about, and we had a lovely picnic, and I thought,
what a long way now, I am from Latvia, and I was kvelling,
you know, beaming with pride, and I said to Hannah, "Hannah
bubele, you know, you're great, the way you are and the way
you understand these things. The other girls." That was the only
time I mentioned it. The other girls.

Hannah didn't say anything. I'm not sure she really heard me.
But that was all that was ever said about it.

BILL: I asked the nurses after she passed, and they said it's rare
enough but some people, when they know they're dying do
want to settle accounts. They want to tell. And Sissy, yes, she
wanted to tell alright. So I got it all, right from the start.

She was lighting one cigarette off the butt of the last. And
croaked on and on. A voice like it was coming out of an old
gramophone. And I tried to make sense of it and wondered
what to believe exactly, and wondered what I was doing here.

I suppose it's just, when people tell you stories about this or
that, well, it's rarely perhaps quite as simple as is made out.
Take the old story 'we were swindled'. 'We thought it was New
York'. 'The captain told us to get off'. I'm not sure I ever really
believed all that. It seems too much like a story. What I think
was this – it was greyer. They were trying to get to New York,
or Canada or South Africa, but a lot of the countries they came
out of wouldn't let them out with more than a certain amount
of money, and they were scared that when they got to the other
end, they wouldn't be let in. Because they were too poor. Or
maybe they were smuggling a bit. Or maybe their paperwork
wasn't in order, a lot of the places these people were coming
from wouldn't even give them a passport. Latvia, Lithuania,
Poland. So in a way, they were the illegal immigrants of their
day and only too ready to jump ship if it got them through.

I'm not in the slightest bit blaming them. They did absolutely the right thing, and they were, as far I can see, brave and adventurous people. When you think of what happened to the people who got left behind. They were right to go. I mean I believe in contracts and the Law – I really do – but when the whole world is a swindle – then sure, cheat.

So I was watching this ashtray fill up – like in a series of photographs, and I guess, something started to wake up, inside.

HANNAH: The first thing I felt was really, really stupid. When he said "the other girls." Lovely beach, lovely sky, two boys playing, open sea all the way to Iceland. Of course, of course. "The other girls". I am not a stupid woman I think, but it had never occurred to me. Were we not husband and wife, and it is written, "You shall not commit adultery", and so that is what I thought.

Yes he was often out. Yes. No, I'm not saying it was not obvious when he said it. That's the point, it was so obvious. It was just that up to then I had completely trusted him. Not even trust – it simply never occurred to me there might be others.

And my own father had worked all hours – he was never home either. That was the division. The men worked, you looked after the home. I no more asked him what he did in the evenings than he asked me what went into borscht.

Can your heart be broken by a man you don't love? It could and it was.

I didn't hate him. If I had loved him and he had done this to me, I think I would have hated him, stabbed him, gone crazy for jealousy. Found the other women, made a terrible scene. But I just felt cold and dead. Because I suddenly just saw him for what he was. A cad. That sounds so inadequate. But that's what he was. I had married the wrong man after all. I had sacrificed my love, for what? My marriage was nothing.

So now fate. Fate came into play.

Two weeks later myself, Lottie, my sister you remember, and Saul were booked into the Ulster Hall. This was before it got turned into a dance hall for the American GIs. Lev and I used to take them out to concerts as a treat. Lev said he would have to work late. Maybe sleep over the shop. And that night Lottie was sick. She couldn't come.

So Saul and I went to the concert alone.

Have you heard Brahms' Symphony Number Three? I started to cry and I held Saul's hand. I held his hand. I don't know what he thought about that, I have no idea.

Afterwards I put on my fur coat and my little fur hat – oh hadn't I done well – and I said, 'Walk me home Saul.'

That night I just decided in my head that Saul was my husband. I just walked along, my arm in his arm, you know exactly as if he was my husband. A real husband that I loved. And we passed under the chestnut trees and along the railings, and it was so nice. We may have talked, I don't know. I just remember his heat and the stars, and the quiet houses with their bay windows all calm.

Well we came to the door, and we went inside, and I asked the maid how had the children been and then I sent her off.

And just as if he was my husband, I said, 'Come to bed now Saul' and I led him upstairs and we made love, in that big bedroom that Lev had provided.

Of course it was a bit odd. I mean it wasn't at all like a romantic film where violins swell and waves crash on the shore. It was physical, that's what it was, it was just the pure fact of holding the man I love inside me. It was the first time a part of me didn't think, 'am I doing this right?', 'is this how it is supposed to be?'

And you know, afterwards you think there are no more secrets then, that you and your lover know everything there is to know – but Saul was still a world to himself. I knew him no more than I had done before. His eyes shone, but what was in there I don't know. I couldn't say I knew Saul any more than I could know what Brahms's music meant. He was music. Well no, that's a bit much perhaps. He was a strange and lovely man, that's all, and he left eventually, and when he went he said, "Hannah, so you know, this will not happen again."

Lev: Well now. A third child on the way! The thing was impossible you understand. It could not be my child – unless the divine had intervened, but we'll leave that sort of thing to the Christians. Hannah and I had not…

Well I went all around the houses on that one. Hannah was a harlot, she had betrayed me, throw her out, curse her! You can imagine.

I remember sitting quietly at the back of the besmedrash, the shul and letting it go round and round and round.

Then I thought – hold on now Lev. What she has done, is it any worse than what you have done yourself? Shall you judge her by a higher standard than yourself? Is that right?

In the end I decided, whatever else I had been I had not been a hypocrite yet. So, so I made my peace with her, as well as I could.

I never asked her who was the father – what did that matter? It's a small community. The Jewish one and the Belfast one. Suppose I had to meet this man every day, and that might have meant a fight or some unpleasantness.

So I asked her plainly, "Is it over?"

And she said "Yes."

And I said, "Hannah, this cannot happen again."

And she said it wouldn't.

And I said well, well, the child will be mine then.

Siss: Great flames in Donegall Square. You remember Disney's *Fantasia*, where the volcano comes to life. We had seen it. Well the flames and the smoke were like that. A great fire dybbuk playing, columns of black in the sky.

And Lev was with his few Dad's Army men, in their helmets, directing useless hoses at the flames in his shop. And he was shouting. I could see his mouth shouting but not hear him. It was so noisy it was as if you were struck deaf by sound.

"Benny, Benny, Benny." Like slow motion.

"Mr Rosen! Come out!" Mr Rosen he called him. His dear friend and partner.

There was the sound of breaking of beams inside. A great cracking and whooomph. And the building sat down like a dog whose ribs are all broken.

And out came Benny, poor dear Benny, out came Mr Rosen and both his arms stopped at the elbow.

Later that night. I think so much later it was light, myself, Mother and Father we sat at the table in our house.

The table was one of Benny's £5 ones he did up for the wedding. Lovely man. Oh he died of course. Father came back, I mean very bitter, from the hospital. It had taken Benny three hours to be seen – and both his hands gone! Well. He wasn't going to survive that. You know you're supposed to say the doctors performed miracles – well maybe they did and maybe they didn't. But a lot of people died waiting, and any fool knew the Germans were coming.

And Daddy was in a rage. I had never seen it in him, what a man, what a great man my father was.

"I am Lev! I am Lev! I will build this all again! I will build this all again!"

How do you judge your own father? The women? The children saved on the farm? Banging his fist on the table all blackened with soot. "I am Lev, I am Lev and I will build this all again."

But he didn't. He died in five years.

For one thing Benny had three sons and that was difficult. You see, they didn't see why they needed Lev. What exactly did he do after all? One of them could keep the books just as well. They tried to do new things too quickly, and it was war-time and even though there was a lot of work needed there wasn't much money around. They updated the designs too. They were ahead of the time in a way, and the 'modern' things that Benny had been making looked very old-fashioned to them, so they made these new pieces that people admired but couldn't afford.

"Give me a plain 3 pound table and I will sell a thousand."

"Give me a plain 3 pound table and I will sell ten thousand."

But the boys wouldn't listen.

Dad had a heart attack in the little flat over his shop and that was that.

Lev: Heart attack with a lovely girl half your age – not so bad. Benny's sons never liked my... arrangement – strange how often the children are more strict than the parents.

And we had the place rebuilt, but the debt was terrible.

My boys were alright, safe in America, but Hannah and Siss, I was worried about them. I was sorry I had nothing to leave, except the house.

Here's a funny thing, Hannah I had done my best by, and if my failings were bad – they were at least the failings of a man and I tried my best not to let her suffer for them. But Sissy – my wife's child. My child. She was very musical, very musical – I was so proud of that.

I remember, before I left, that she and Saul sang at my funeral – special permission was given for a woman to sing.

They sing: [*Psalm for the dead – uplifting and moving – El Maleh Rakhamim*].

I liked that. It was a send-off alright. Not bad I thought, Lev, you're a long way from Latvia now.

But I worried about Siss.

Hannah: When did I tell her that she wasn't Lev's? Well, I didn't.

But I did tell the boys.

Oh, look I suppose I made a dreadful mess of it all, and I didn't know what I was doing – or if I did know I was always too much of a coward to face it. I sacrificed my daughter's life for mine so help me, and I will not be forgiven.

Lev died in 1946, and it was, I think, about six months after that, when the shipping was safe again, that the boys came over to help settle the affairs. It was very messy because of the debts. I didn't understand it at all – neither my father nor Lev ever expected me to understand paperwork, so I expect I made a mess of that too – at least that's what the boys seemed to think.

We were up late one evening and I felt they were in a way belittling their father – I don't want to speak ill of my sons – but they were criticising the way he had done things. The fact that the business had vanished. It was like they were picking him apart and he couldn't answer for himself, and it was going around and around – and I remember there was a receipt that they couldn't find and somehow this was Lev's fault, so something inside me burst and I said, "You don't know anything about your father." And I just had to tell them. I told them how he had never blamed me and how he accepted Sissy as his own. I didn't mention his other women you know, because I wanted them to think well of him.

"You criticise this man because you can't find some fiddly receipt – I carried Lev's own brother's daughter and he forgave me and never said one cross word."

I tell you, there was a bit of a silence after that.

Then they shouted and roared and called me all sorts of things. Lev never did that, but the boys – oh it was terrible. I was still their mother!

And they said when she asks for a dowry – you tell her what you did and why she'll get nothing. And I didn't really understand why my sin was her fault too, but somehow it was. Or perhaps I had mean sons, and it suited them not to pay.

But I never did have the nerve to tell her. I mean when do you find a suitable day to tell?

Siss: Belfast in the 1950s. I had a very enjoyable time.

Churchill made that awful speech about, what was it, the dreary, grey spires of Ulster? – but it wasn't at all like that.

I supported both Mother and me as a piano teacher and took up smoking – which was rather risqué for a single woman.

I had a bicycle and I went around, smoking and teaching and going to concerts. And I helped get the new shul built. I was on the committee. Yorke, Rosenberg and Merdall designed it, and I like the way they kept it very light. I took the notes sometimes and Barney Hurwitz, he was a funny man, he would say, Siss, let's listen carefully to every point of view at the meeting, and after – let's you and me decide what the notes say. That was the way he got things done.

It cost £80,000 and we opened without owing a penny. Barney Hurwitz OBE was not an easy man to say no to. And he did it without putting plaques all over the place. I was pleased we were all in the same space too – not like the old shul.

So for most of the time I was happy.

I had a good time with the music too – partly by staying a bit out of the community. Remember I said that Rose – my skipping friend – had a brother called Jim. He used to lend me records. The trad scene was having its revival at the time and I got interested in that. I was there when the McPeakes started up. I bought an Arran sweater. I expect you know this, but the piano for traditional music is really a rhythmic accompaniment. Not too difficult, and the tunes you know are very close – Yiddish and Irish. Mother didn't really like that, because her life was about getting away from all that Yiddish stuff, which she thought was common and old-fashioned. Her idea of music was Chopin and a fur coat.

Anyway, I nagged and nagged at Jim until he sort of asked for me, and then it was arranged that I could go down to a certain house. And we had to knock at the window. I thought it was all an adventure, but Jim was white-faced about it. The sessions were great. I can't tell you. There was a dusty old upright in the parlour and I sat in. Yes, I used to sit in with the McPeakes – now and then. "I'll tell me Ma". "Will ye go Lassie Go." Francy sang that for his sweetheart, after she left him. He was very broken over that.

There was a fiddle player called Larry Shaw – from Dundalk originally and if I ever had a lover it was him. Not that we did anything of course. I was forty by then and he was twenty-five, though that wouldn't have bothered Lev.

We played together. I think when someone is properly musical that's the best part of them. It's in the music. So when two people really play together, well that's the best of them and the best of you creating something together. It's very intimate – because it's a conversation too. Of course you don't talk about these things because that would ruin it. And very inarticulate too these trad people. But Larry and I... well we knew and that's what counted. He married a nice girl called Elaine – very artistic, and the two of them went to Dublin when times got bad and that was that.

Why didn't I go?

Mother.

I would have gone if I hadn't had to look after her. I was always good at French and I thought I might go off to Paris and teach piano there. I wouldn't say the '70s here were as bad as the second world war. But it was bad enough, and a lot of people did go – because it's hard to make a living in a city at war with itself.

And I have to be clear, the blitz was much, much more frightening. But the city turned in on itself, became smaller, and it was constant, it never seemed to be over. I think because it was nearly normal so much of the time, that made the violence, the bombs, so much worse. There were times when people would whisper, maybe not to go near that shop or don't be seen at the front door there and you couldn't really cross the street.

But I had to look after Mother, and she wouldn't go because Saul and Lottie were here and they wouldn't go because Saul liked the acoustics of the new shul – here, and he sang until he was nearly ninety.

Hannah was sick from the day Lev died. No – from the day her sons left, that was it, until the day she died, which was over forty years later.

I never married because I had no dowry and I had a sick mother. I was no longer a catch. Mother wrote to the boys, but nothing. I was very bitter about that and cut them off from my mind. Though I kept in touch with their children, because I thought you can't blame children for the faults of the parents, so I sent them little gifts for Bar mitzvahs and things like that.

But the community... it sort of shrank. Dan and Esther Levy still chatted away in the delicatessen, but you know, there wasn't the trade. Then one of the butchers went and then the other – I think Nemtzov was last.

Thank goodness for *Countdown*. It was never the same after that poor Richard Whiteley died, but in the early days it was great. Right to the end, when she couldn't remember her own name and thought we were living in Leeds, Mum could still do the letters and the numbers. A whizz at the Conundrum she was. She could see it sort of all at once, which I never could.

So finally she died, and at the age of sixty years old I found myself alone and, after the years mourning, free at last.

And the funny thing was, I buried Mother, and thought, I wonder if I should marry? At sixty! Why not? I was free after all.

Lev: My boys. The boys who left me, just as myself and Saul once left my father. Isn't that what we fathers want – that our boys should grow strong and wealthy and have children, and do what we did in their turn?

I liked money because I could have nice suits and eat out, and Hannah could have her coats, and Sissy could have her piano. I liked money because Saul could express his gift and there would always be something for him.

But my boys, I think, just liked money. Somehow, I think, men like me and my father were good at setting our boys up, but not so good at reaching into their hearts.

At least my boys would make sure there was a dowry for Sissy wouldn't they – make sure this gifted child could live a full life and make her music. This little girl that when she thought her Daddy was in danger ran all the way from Annesley Street, through the fires to Donegall Square to save her Daddy. Oh yes, Sissy was my girl alright. And I loved her. I am Lev, and the great pride of my life is Sissy, my daughter, Ruth.

End Section 2.

[Saul*prostrateshimselfandsingssongofatonement.Possiblyothers join in.*]

Section 3. *Forgiveness.*

Bill: By the way her real name wasn't Sissy. It was just that she had the two brothers and they called her Sister, which became Sissy.

They were very good in the hospice. Great. I'm booked into the Europa, but I never made it there. I'm still in the clothes I arrived in. They let me sleep in the chair, when I could.

Remember I said Siss came over for my wedding, that's how we'd met. I knew she'd fallen out with my grandfather, but you know I never asked what that was all about. I mean, I've known whole families torn apart when someone's aunt cheated at bridge. I didn't dig into it.

Turns out Hannah had left a will. And in that will everything went to Sissy and nothing to her two brothers. Now, you'd think this was because the two boys, who were nearly seventy and with apartments in Miami, needed nothing, and Sissy who had cared for Hannah for forty years, did. That's what Sissy thought. Well, you'd also think that the two boys would let it go. But they didn't. They flew over and contested. They contested on the grounds that Sissy was not Lev's daughter and that they had only been allowing the property to rest in Hannah's keeping as Lev's wife, and now she was gone, it should revert to them. They walked into the house they hadn't been in for forty years with the piano they couldn't play, and told Sissy to her face, what her mother had never dared. What frikkin' momzers. $15! It offended me badly, because a will is a contract too, and these guys were really only acting like maggots to see if Sissy could be bullied into settling out of court. If they made it unpleasant. Well they did that alright.

But Sissy wouldn't budge.

Sissy said there was no proof, the birth cert said Lev – this was before DNA testing – and anyway she was Hannah's daughter after all, and it was Hannah's house to give. She said it was like an out of body thing, because they were screaming at each other, and at the same moment they said it, her life made absolute sense and a part of her was somehow meditating over it. They called it incest. She felt like a light was shining all around her. Horrible as the way it came out or not, she understood herself at last.

So she booted them out. And then she said she'd liked the look of me at the wedding and she repeated, the sins of the parents should not be on the children, and the child should not blame her parents either. Siss, at the very end, took responsibility for her own life. She said, of course her mother should have told her, but it had been her life, and what she had done with it, she had done, and she regretted nothing, and Hannah no doubt had her reasons and who is to know the secrets of the human heart. It was a big thing to take her life back for herself. And she meant it too.

I said I'm not a complex man inside. I don't think I am but, um, some things kind of get through.

Watching someone pass. It's like nothing else. For one thing, at the last Sissy didn't want to die. When it comes to it, who does? And it's not easy. It's noisy and it's stressful and it's exhausting and in the end it's astonishing.

Afterwards I went to the house – for the first time. She had given me the keys, it was all arranged.

Stepping into the actual house was weird. It was both just like you'd imagine and nothing like it. Benny's table was there. And the piano. And upstairs the bedroom, the one where Hannah and Saul had made love. So like stepping into the story I guess.

But you could see Sissy had got old there too. She must have been sleeping downstairs. There was just ash and butts everywhere. All over the tables, the piano. The ceilings were yellow. I guess she felt the cold too, as there were two of those heaters you can wheel around the place.

So I thought things through.

I'm a pretty organised guy, so I knew to phone the Rabbi, solicitor. I wondered whether I'd be counted as one of the minyan. I was actually, they might have disapproved of me, but they couldn't have been nicer.

Lev, Sissy, Hannah, Saul ....who am I to judge. Do I have the right to say this was a good thing to do, this a bad? So and so is a good person, so and so was wicked.

What can you say. That they lived. They were here. They did the best they could do in the time they were in.

When I come to the end of my days, and my story is told, will I abide the account? But I have no desire to get to the end of my days yet.

The short of it is – I've told myself downsizing to New Jersey isn't so bad and I've enough to get through. I've decided to do Sissy's house up and sell it. And I've arranged to put the money in a fund for the elderly, so they might be a little more secure in their passing.

That doesn't make me a good man though. It just seems that, okay, I have something inside me now that isn't a contract and isn't a duty, but a feeling. Interesting, I must try some more of them. Actually, I really want to talk to my wife now. Not on the phone either.

Y'know you can't put right what was done wrong. Atonement, that's too big for me. But you can do the decent thing.

Now I'm going to the airport. I'm going to have a grande latte. And go home. In the same suit.

The Gates of Prayer are now closed.

[*Closing prayer – Ne'ilah, the closing prayer.* SAUL *leads all apart from* BILL *one way,* SISSY *being welcomed and given pride of place.* BILL *puts his shoes on and leaves like a normal guy.*]

The End

The Lamplighters
by Jo Egan

In April 2008 as Creative Producer of Kabosh, I began interviewing members of the Belfast Hebrew Community as part of the Jewish Memory Project: a Kabosh initiative. 42 participants took part: 23 living in Northern Ireland and a further 19 now living throughout England. The following extracts are from the oral archive which will be officially presented to the Belfast Hebrew Community by Kabosh later this year.

'My Grandfather was one of four brothers and they lived in a village called Telsiai in Lithuania and they decided, when the pogroms started – and also because they wanted to better themselves, they decided to go to the States. So they bought four tickets for the boat, this is around 1880, and they arrived where they thought was New York but actually was only Liverpool. And that was where they had to get off. So they only had enough money between the four of them to buy three tickets so they drew lots and my Grandfather lost.' – Edwin Coppel

These stories tell an incredible tale of a raggle-taggle community which started arriving in Belfast and Lurgan around 1880. These refugees settled in the streets around Carlisle Circus in the triangle formed by the Crumlin Road and the Old Lodge Road.

My first interviewee was Harold Ross, by practice the community's memory-keeper.

'Why did your Grandfather settle in Northern Ireland?' I asked, wanting a step-by-step.

'We came to make Parnose: the means of earning a livelihood' Meshine mokem, meshane mazl – *'New place, new luck'.*

And he was right. The simple fact was that whoever ended up here for whatever reason did so because they heard there was a living to be had. Brother followed brother, uncles paid for nephews. They in turn brought their family and the chain extended, sometimes through marriage, sometimes by word of mouth; a familiar tale for all of us on this island.

Ways of earning a living ranged from selling door-to-door, credit retailing, cabinet making and of course tailoring. I interviewed Steven Jaffe in his London office, his Great-Grandfather had originally come to Belfast from Lublin in Poland. He has completed an exhaustive study on the Belfast Jewish Community soon to be published. He told me,

'In the beginning the standard way of making a living was day-to-day peddling going door-to-door, not just in Belfast. There could hardly have been a town or a street where a Jewish peddler wasn't walking down with his pack...some would sell holy pictures and pictures of King Billy crossing the Boyne – so very early on they would have to know which door they were knocking on.'

The original Jewish Community in Belfast, dating from 1864, was comprised of twenty-five families; mostly well-heeled German merchants, who were key players in the linen and shipbuilding industries. The original Jewish community in Belfast, dating from 1864, was comprised of twenty-five families; mostly well -heeled German merchants, key players in the linen and shipbuilding industry.

Otto Jaffe was probably the most remarkable character of the time, becoming Lord Mayor of Belfast twice, one of those years being 1904 when at the same time in Limerick the rabid Father Creagh, perched in pulpit, provoked anti-Semitic riots and a boycott of Jewish trade. Sir Otto Jaffe was a well respected businessman and philanthropist until WWI. As the war progressed widespread anti-German feeling arose from the use of poisonous gas in the trenches and the sinking of the Luisitania. His peers began to avoid him; there were whispers of espionage and eventually there were objections to Otto's membership on the board of the Children's Hospital - all this, despite the fact that both his son and his nephew were in the British Army. Eventually, in June 1916, Otto Jaffe resigned from Belfast Corporation. He left Belfast and died in London in

1929.

The second influx, arriving in the 1880s, was almost the complete opposite.

Ronnie Appleton remembers,

'The ones who came from Eastern Europe were very religious and very poor. I mean they came with nothing. I remember Morris Sullivan who became a multi-millionaire showing me in Donaghadee, 'Do you see that window? I took a room there at a shilling a week when I was eleven years of age and I went around the countryside selling matches and needles.' They didn't even speak the language. They had to learn the language – no formal English education. They spoke Yiddish. And they had a hard time of it.'

This new influx of refugees followed the Lithuanian tradition which was extremely orthodox. Early on they established a Chevra Gemorah (1885), a place of learning dedicated to the study of the oral law of the Talmud. Men attended either before or after a day's work and for many it was the high point of the day. According to Steven Jaffe,

'They would study Talmud on a page to page basis, each day Strong personalities led the Gemorah class...it tended to be a lay member, Chaim Weinstein...it was said that he used to teach with his eyes shut because he knew the Talmud so well. The way of studying Gemorah is by argument. The Talmud itself is a series of arguments between Rabbis who lived in the first century onwards and they are constantly arguing and therefore it's a dialectic. The essence of it is in the argument rather than the conclusion. It's a thinking thing rather than a clear yes or no.'

As individual wealth grew the community began to move up the Antrim Road. A denied membership to Salisbury Tennis Club led to the foundation of the Jewish Institute in Ashfield Gardens in 1927. It became the centre of Jewish social life and had tennis courts, a debating society, visiting speakers, weekly bridge and card games, a kosher restaurant and a ballroom occupying the whole of the upper floor hosting the annual New Year's ball as well as weekly hops. Gerald Wainer spoke of this time with enthusiasm,

'I went to what was called the Junior Forum, which was a debating society where we had 50 to 60 young people talking about balloon debates, talking about different subjects. Young men that went on to become top barristers stood up for the first time and spoke in public.'

In 1904 Sir Otto Jaffe had built a new Synagogue at Annesley St replacing the original site on Great Victoria St which dated from 1869. In the mid-1950s the community was at its apex and there was needed a larger and more conveniently placed Synagogue. The then President of the community, Barney Hurwitz, was described as a human dynamo, dedicated to fundraising. Each Sunday he collected donations from as little as 10 shillings to £10,000. Ivan Selig was the Secretary for the community at the time and worked closely beside Barney Hurwitz:

'Barney Hurwitz would phone and say, 'I'd like to come and have a cup of coffee with you', that was his entry ticket, and he would come and have a cup of coffee with you and take money off you, and he collected all the money personally, and the shul was open free of debt, which was quite remarkable.'

The opening ceremony was in 1964. The Synagogue was packed to the rafters. It was the high point of this community's 85 years in Belfast. As it happened, it was all downhill from there.

Gerald Wainer grew up aware of the opportunities his parents and others had created:

'Our parents' generation didn't have the chances that we had. And they really worked hard to give us those chances. To them the ideal was to have a profession because a profession meant that little piece of paper was an insurance policy. And they never

had that chance. In our generation a very large portion of young people had a university education.'

The only thing I was told that might be construed as anti-Semitic wasn't actually that, merely straightforward discrimination. Graduates in medicine spoke of the plumb jobs going to indigenous Protestants. The 50's saw many young people looking further afield, tempted by opportunities offered beyond Northern Ireland. This was a natural progression. Those that continued education and training elsewhere might have returned with young families but the outbreak of the Troubles in 1969 further shook the structure – established families with businesses now contemplated leaving. The first family to leave Northern Ireland as a direct result of the Troubles left in 1972. Now thirty-seven years later as Eta and Gerald Wainer relayed their experience, Eta clearly became upset:

'Gerald and I were involved in a very bad bomb scare in the Slieve Donard Hotel. That's when, really, I think we just felt we couldn't take it any more.

And, when we said we were going people were horrified. They couldn't believe it. They said, 'Don't be ridiculous. This'll all blow over in a year. What are you running away for?' And, unfortunately, we were proved right. Often, they followed suit some years later.

I never forget the night we left, the people that came down to the boat to see us off. It was just absolutely...heart-rending and heart-warming. Nobody wanted us to go.'

Gerald continued:

'I sold a business, a thriving business about 100 yards from the first health centre in Northern Ireland with nine doctors in it, and I had built that pharmacy up from four bare walls and, very often, over a long period of time, doing very little. And it was then that I would have been reaping the rewards, and I sold that business for virtually nothing.

Everybody knew us. Everybody knew my Grandparents. My grandfather was a very religious man, and everybody knew who he was, and my Grandmother. They knew my parents at our shop.

When we first came here (Bournemouth), our friends, that we eventually made, thought we were mad. We used to get a babysitter just to walk around the town centre and look in the shop windows – because we hadn't had that freedom.'

Whole families started leaving, often taking widowed grandparents with them.

When I commenced the oral archive, eighty per cent of the community was over sixty.

Currently there are approximately 100 members left of the Belfast Jewish Community.

At its height there were approximately 2,000 members.

Following the Belfast interviews I travelled to England to interview a further nineteen people that had left Northern Ireland between the years 1962–2008. I had presumed the community that does Exodus would have had so many leavings that upheaval would be second nature. For some who had left Belfast to attend university and stayed away the transition wasn't difficult. But the families born here who had left during the Troubles and after, struck me as devastated. All of them had now re-established their livelihoods, all successfully, and spoke with affection of the strong Jewish communities they had now joined. Yet each family spoke of the difference…How hard it had been to leave and the grief at separation following the move. One parent spoke of feeling suicidal, …the sense of a large family becoming fragmented and the resulting overwhelming sense of loss. The following sentiments were expressed again and again:

'We can never replace what we had there. We're not fully at

home here. I miss the sound of the accent on the streets. We grew up in such a happy environment.'

Back home in Belfast when I interviewed Denis Coppel he said:

'But nothing ever stays the same. Things move on. You can't live in the past.

We had a man here, a Rabbi a few years ago and he talked about the small communities. And he said the average life of a small community is a hundred years. We've now survived for more than a hundred years. So we're coming up to our sell-by date. And I think it's irreversible because we don't have any new people coming in and the people here are getting old and they're dying.'

It's been an incredible journey to observe. It's easy to track how the emphasis on learning, the support of the Jewish Institute, the importance of the third level education pushed each generation forward, perhaps to a place where Northern Ireland became too provincial.

Despite the early poverty, the dedication to religious practice, to a way of thinking, provided a structure which enabled future generations not just to aspire to the piece of paper but the ability to absorb and engage with the learning.

Harold Ross died some months following his interview. He told me:

'We are supposed to be lamplighters – we're supposed to light the light to bring back the light of Torah here. When you're speaking say, 'Harold is a lamplighter here.'

Kol Isha -
The Voice of a Woman
by Katy Radford

This Is What We Sang began with a chance encounter some three years ago at a photographic exhibition, when Kabosh director Paula McFetridge and I discussed the possibility of producing a site-specific play in the synagogue at the Wolfson Centre in North Belfast. We began from the premise that the Jewish Community in Belfast (in keeping with other Jewish communities throughout the world) is a success story of the survival, against the odds, of a people living in diaspora, with all the frailties of being human brings. The history of the Belfast Jewish Community provides a pertinent reminder of the need to ensure that minority communities, new migrants and those who are marginalised (including women) are given the opportunity to participate fully in the economic, social and cultural life of Northern Ireland. And as with our non-Jewish neighbours, friends and relatives, the word Community for Jews is not an easy concept, covering as it does a multitude of expectations, aspirations and restrictions.

Today the community's collective life centres around the synagogue and to ensure that those who are most observant can participate fully in all activities there, it is an Orthodox *shul* providing an umbrella to all who are interested in Jewish culture from within the framework of *Halacha* – Jewish law that provides the benchmark for Orthodox life. In Belfast women are welcomed as members of the Executive Council and attend services, but there are certain *mitzvot* (commandments) that we are unable to perform here, with different roles and obligations prescribed on the basis of gender.

Numbers of Jewish people in the North have reduced to almost a tenth of what they were at their peak. Many women have chosen to continue their education and build family life in other places where they find it easier to explore and pursue experiences from within Jewish traditions. This is, in part, due to what it is now fashionable to refer to as organisational anti-Semitism, namely the processes of direct and in-direct discrimination being embedded into the fabric of public, private and voluntary life and that in turn impact on how people have been able to access culturally appropriate goods and services. A poignant example of this is how the community's last Rabbi and Rebbetzin left when their children came to school-age so that they might be educated in a way that enabled them to engage fully in what they described as a Jewish way of life.

The process of creating *This Is What We Sang* was slow. And rightly so. A number of people from the community became involved in discussions with the theatre company to ensure that the content, narrative and production value would be something appropriate for the venue and would be a welcome foundation stone in the programme of the Community's *'Jews Schmooze'* arts initiative. Kabosh recognised that to secure the support of the community, engaging the community in the development of the entire process would be key and in order for the writer and director to get a sense of the Jewish experience in Ireland, considerable research would need to be undertaken. Jo Egan worked closely with the then Chairman, Edwin Coppel, to identify potential contributors to the research process and began to compile an oral history archive of existing and former members spending many weeks travelling throughout Ireland and England recording the experiences they wanted to share. Their narratives were given to the author Gavin Kostick to consider as he developed his fictitious version of one family's experiences since the 19th century. To ensure the community had an opportunity to comment on the developing play, Kabosh organised a reading of the first draft for the President, Chair and members of the Executive Council of the Community. And the cast and key crew members were welcomed at services and social events to help them prepare for their performances.

Women indisputably play an integral part in Jewish life and the continuation of traditions. There are many ongoing debates that continue to evolve about the public and private roles of women in Jewish society: matrilineal descent, conversion in and out of the religion, *niddah* and *mikvah* (issues of purificiation and cleanliness) have all been used to both create conflict and forge agreement within and across families and communities. One of those issues is referred to in passing within the play but needed much consideration in its production, namely the concept of *Kol Isha*, the prohibition in Orthodox Judaism of men hearing women sing. In a nutshell, this is derived from a quotation taken from the Song of Solomon, "Let me hear your voice, for your voice is sweet (*arev*) and your face is beautiful." By way of a very brief and unscholarly explanation, the prohibition was first raised by those interpreters for whom the translation of *arev* is complicated because its root is compatible with that of the word *ervah* which means nakedness. And consequently, there are some who consider the voice of women in song to be a revelation too intimate to be appropriate for hearing in public. A crucial component of the community's contribution to the development of the play was to consider the role that music both sacred and secular might play in the script and performance. Given the sensitivities and nuances that music can bring to all our lives in Ireland and Britain, and perhaps particularly so in relations between communities, it was crucial that the music for this play was not simply an add-on, or accompaniment. And to that end it was our privilege to welcome back to the synagogue Neil Martin, who has worked with us over a number of years as choirmaster (for the all-male choir). As our North Belfast neighbour, his addition to Kabosh's creative team ensured that the community's interests and musical heritage in all its 'ish'-ness (Jewish, Irish and British) were well represented by someone we might even start to consider an honorary Jew!